a. j. casson

a. j. casson

canadian artists 1

margaret gray
margaret rand
lois steen

gage publishing

Gage Publishing
Copyright Margaret Gray, Margaret Rand, Lois Steen, 1976

Canadian Cataloguing in Publication Data

Gray, Margaret Blair
    A. J. Casson

(Canadian art series (Agincourt, Ont.); no. 1)

    Bibliography: p. 57
    ISBN 0-7715-9962-5
    1. Casson, Alfred Joseph, 1898-
    I. Rand, Margaret, 1918-   II. Steen, Lois.
    III. Title.   IV. Series.
    ND249.C33G73   759.11   C76-017083-5

List of Illustrations

Preface

There are a number of fine Canadian artists who emerged just after the Group of Seven and who have been to a great extent overshadowed by the almost hypnotic public concentration on the spectacular Group. These artists, born within a decade of the turn of the century, are still producing today and we believe they deserve greater recognition.

We are not attempting to make comparisons between artists or judgments about them. Instead, we have set out to acquaint Canadians with artists who have made, and continue to make, important contributions to our national heritage. We have visited them in their homes and these biographies are based on personal interviews in which they have told us about their lives, what they consider significant events and influences and the circumstances under which some of their works came into being. We have freely used direct quotations. How better could we express the artist's own ideas?

A. J. Casson is a friendly, helpful man. He assisted us in every possible way, ferreted out information for us and even allowed us to photograph, step-by-step, the development of a painting from oil sketch to finished canvas. He also rounded up a number of his paintings from private collectors so that we could photograph them, together with Cassons' own collection, in his home.

We spent several pleasant afternoons with Dr. Casson and his wife in the living room of their comfortable Toronto house surrounded by a garden which shows the same hard work and meticulous care that characterize his paintings. He reminisced about his early years, his friends, his successes and disappointments, and the problems that faced an artist trying to survive in the days before the Canada Council was formed. His memory is remarkable but he would occasionally break off and turn to his wife: "What was that fellow's name, Marg?" or "When was it we took that holiday...?" And Margaret would fill in the gap.

In our search for Casson's paintings, many private collectors invited us into their homes and allowed us to photograph their paintings. Some of them prefer to remain anonymous, but they have been, without exception, gracious and helpful. To all of them we say a very sincere thank you.

We also wish to acknowledge with thanks the co-operation of the number of businesses, institutions and art galleries: National Gallery of Canada; Art Gallery of Ontario; Art Gallery of Hamilton; London Public Library & Art Museum; Historical Museum of the Twenty, Jordan, Ontario; Hart House, University of Toronto; Victoria University, Toronto; Toronto-Dominion Bank; We would also like to thank Ron & Ron Design Consultants, Art Gallery of Ontario, Photo Services for the use of their photographs. Their courtesy and interest are much appreciated.

Margaret Gray
Margaret Rand
Lois Steen

A. J. Casson

It was December, 1912. A young boy stood with his back to the class, drawing a Christmas scene with coloured chalk on the blackboard, while a solemn George V looked down from the yellow wall. The boy was fourteen-year-old Alfred Joseph Casson, and he was used to standing in front of the class. The teacher, recognizing his unusual talent, often asked him to teach the art lesson because he was, quite simply, better than she was. He enjoyed doing it and his classmates liked the break in the monotony of the school day, but neither he nor they could guess that this was the beginning of a distinguished career in art which is still continuing after more than sixty years.

Born before the turn of the century, A. J. Casson looks back on a long and satisfying lifetime of painting, during which he has combined those early traits of leadership and artistic talent to carve for himself a significant place in the Canadian art world. Today he is still doing the work he loves, his creativity and skill undiminished, and the demand for his work greater than ever.

Between the years 1920 and 1976, Canadian painting has experienced a series of revolutions, but through them Casson's clear rational style has moved steadily forward. He has been the acceptable bridge spanning the various rebel groups. Even in the turbulent art scene of the twenties, he managed to maintain a balanced course, a member at the same time of the "blasphemous" Group of Seven and of the ultra-conservative Ontario Society of Artists. The eruptions of avant-garde groups over the years have not diverted him from his calm middle path.

His leadership in the years after the breakup of the Group of Seven, his unprejudiced judgment in assessing the work of others, his critical self-evaluation and maintenance of the highest standards for his own work, have made him highly respected. He has worked closely with the police, using his expertise to expose fraudulent art. He has been honoured by his colleagues and by his country. Yet he remains a peaceable, approachable, unassuming man and artist.

A. J. Casson was born in Toronto on 17 May, 1898, to an English Quaker father and a Canadian mother. The family moved to Guelph when Alfred was nine and here he was able to roam the countryside learning to know and love the rocks, trees and streams he would later paint. His upbringing was strict and frugal, with the emphasis on the basic Quaker values of scrupulous honesty, personal integrity and hard work combined with painstaking thoroughness. These characteristics, imprinted on the boy, have remained fundamental to the man and his work.

As far back as he can remember, Alfred loved to draw but his hands were clever in other ways too.

"There was nothing in Guelph in those days," he recalls. "You had to make your own amusements. I took manual training at school and found I had an aptitude for tools. So I made all kinds of things — Punch and Judy shows, furniture for my mother, cages and hutches for my pet animals."

Even then, he was capable of seeing what had to be done and adapting the materials at hand to do the job. He could fit his ideas and designs to the conditions and circumstances — an ability he perfected later in his commercial art work.

When Casson was fourteen, the family moved to Hamilton, and it was there that his formal art training began at Hamilton "Tech." At fifteen he got his first job with Laidlow Lithographing Co. where he worked long hours at the menial jobs of sweeping and cleaning, only occasionally being allowed to try his hand at design. Then, for two years, he was employed at Commercial Engravers, where he thoroughly learned the process of engraving and reproduction — useful training for his future career as a commercial artist.

Four years later the family moved to Toronto and the loose threads began to come together to form the fabric of Casson's career. In a small exhibition in the local library he saw the works of Tom Thomson, Arthur Lismer, A. Y. Jackson and, excited by their approach to landscape, he began to haunt the ravines of Toronto to sketch and paint. He continued his art studies in the evenings at Central Technical School, where a dedicated teacher, Alfred Howell, praised his early efforts and encouraged him to develop his talent for landscape painting. He also studied with Harry Britton, a fine artist, who taught him the principles of the restricted palette which he uses to this day.

A. J. Casson was first publicly exhibited at the Canadian National Exhibition in 1917. He was just nineteen, and his friend Fred Haines, who was in charge of the C.N.E. Gallery, came round to see him. The gallery mainly imported the shows of American or British artists and there was only one small room of Canadian art. Casson was lucky to have one of his paintings chosen as it was not an open exhibition to which artists could submit their work.

At that time the opportunities for Canadian artists to exhibit their works were severely limited. The National Gallery had been founded in 1880 to be a repository for diploma works of the successful applicants to the Royal Canadian Academy. After 1920, it began slowly to build up a collection of established Canadian artists, but its small and uncertain annual budget for acquisitions could not be counted on for support of young unknown talent. Unlike today, when hundreds of small galleries are exhibiting new as well as established artists, the few private galleries that existed would show only the well-known. There was a gallery at Eaton's, and one or two picture-framing dealers, but they exhibited only paintings by artists of whom their clientele might have heard. Art was not something in which the average man thought of investing his hard-earned savings, and so it was a very limited market.

A painter could submit his work to the Ontario Society of Artists for the exhibition in the spring. When it came back, he could send it to the Academy in Montreal in the fall. After that he had exhausted his opportunities for showing it. Very few artists in Canada could support themselves solely by their art. It is not surprising that Casson was well into his thirties before it occurred to him that he could one day become a full-time professional painter.

At the end of World War I, Casson "floundered around for a while" after he got out of the Air Force but then, at the age of twenty-one, he was set on the course from which he never looked back:

I was lucky, I know. In 1919, through a friend of my mother's, I heard there was a job at Rous & Mann. I applied and got it. They were printers and they were superior to anyone in Canada. If you went under Mr. Robson in the art department, you immediately put on a bowler hat and had it made. You were the elite!

He found himself at a desk beside an artist named Frank Carmichael (one of the original Group of Seven) who had a profound influence on his development.

Frank and I hit it off well. He was tough, but he taught me how to paint. And he took me to the Arts & Letters Club where the whole Group of Seven used to meet every day at noon. It just opened the door for me. I say it was luck. I wasn't pushing it, but there was the opportunity and I had common-sense enough to make use of it.

Luck, in the sense that Casson was in the right place at the right time, was certainly on his side. But his serious approach to work, instilled in him by his Quaker heritage, was an important element. And without his fine talent and obvious integrity, he would not have been accepted into the company of the Group of Seven, since there was a real generation gap. He was eight years younger than his friend Frank, who was himself the youngest of the Group, and twenty-seven years junior to J. E. H. MacDonald. Cass recalls:

It all goes back to Grip Ltd., where Ab Robson was the Art Director and had nearly the whole Group of Seven working for him. Jim MacDonald was senior artist. Varley was there, and Frank Johnston and Tom Thomson — not Harris or Jackson, and I don't think Lismer. Frank Carmichael was the office boy. Then when Rous & Mann formed, Robson went over as partner and Art Director.

All of the Group, with the exception of Lawren Harris, had to support themselves initially as teachers or commercial artists. But the designation "commercial" was considered a pejorative one, and they left the commercial field as soon as they could.

"When I first went into commercial work," Casson says, "there was a stigma about it. I know of a very well-known water colourist in Toronto who was put up for the Academy—there wasn't a finer water colourist in the Academy. He was turned down, and afterwards I heard an academician say, 'He's no painter. He's a commercial man.'"

Casson and Carmichael had family responsibilities (Casson supported his widowed mother) and could not escape to the uncertainties of "freedom." And, as Frank Carmichael told Cass, "In this country an artist has three choices open to him: he can teach, he can go commercial — or he can starve!"

Casson does not regret the disciplined, commercial training and experience. They taught him his simplified, uncluttered approach to composition, the clean, clear colours which have become his hallmark. It was creative work, within its limits. He enjoyed doing it — and he had to eat.

I got a wonderful training at Rous & Mann. It was the top place in Canada. When I went in, it was just like a fifteen-year-old being made a member of the Royal Academy in England. But then Frank moved to Samson-Matthews and I realized my work was narrowing to very fine, specialized assignments — beautiful things, but I was getting into a rut. Then I had this chance to go to Samson-Matthews, where there were posters, books, display work, lots of variety. I talked it over with Frank and he told me if I

A. J. Casson, Lawren Harris, A. Y. Jackson and F. H. Varley (*left to right*)

*wanted to develop, here was my chance. Rous &
Mann are still tops in their field, but it's a very
narrow field.*

He remained with Samson-Matthews until
his retirement thirty-two years later as
Vice-President and Art Director when, at the age
of sixty, he at last felt free to become a full-time
painter.

In the early years Casson and Carmichael used to
drive up north to paint every weekend in Frank's
old "Bell" — a car made in his father's carriage
shop in Orillia.

*We'd stay overnight in an old hotel on Friday, get
up at 7 Saturday morning and go to Severn
Bridge and paint all day and all day Sunday, and
we'd get home to Toronto about 9 P.M. Mrs.
Carmichael would give us our dinner and then
Frank would have a hundred and one things for
me to see, and about twelve midnight I'd pry
myself away and catch the radial car on Yonge
Street to the city limits (now Summerhill) then
the Yonge car, then the Bloor car. I'd get home
about 3 A.M. and have to be at work the next
morning by 8 A.M. But if I didn't do that, Frank
wouldn't have anything to do with me.*

The friendship of the two men developed
steadily and they went out together sketching at

every opportunity. Eventually Carmichael's
influence was so strong that Casson had to break
away from the older man in order to establish his
own style.

In 1921 Casson began to receive some
recognition. Frank persuaded him to submit
work to the Ontario Society of Artists and it was
accepted for exhibition. He became a member of
the O.S.A. in 1923 and also began showing
regularly with the Royal Canadian Academy. The
National Gallery purchased his painting *The
Clearing*. He was on his way! He was still not a
member of the Group of Seven, but he went out
painting with them as often as he could and he
was infected with the excitement of their new
ideas.

A. J. Casson married in 1924, and his wife
Margaret has quietly lent him encouragement
and support, sharing his triumphs and
disappointments for over fifty years. Earlier that
year, Casson had a fall while skating that
activated a kidney stone and resulted in the
doctor's dictum, "No sketching outdoors for a
year." He soon found an alternative in the
greenhouses of Allen Gardens and he went there
every weekend to paint flowers. In these still
lifes, his unerring colour sense and fine
brushwork show that he could have made a name
for himself in this field. An avid gardener, he has
always loved flowers, but at the end of the year

"Old Bell"

he turned his back on them as subject matter for his paintings and again took up landscape.

PETUNIAS
Casson spent a year partly immobilized by an accident. During this time he painted a series of small panels of flowers and still lifes. These paintings glow with spontaneous splashes of clear colour in the fashion of the older artists with whom he had painted: Carmichael, Jackson, Harris.

Collection of Mr. & Mrs. C. A. G. Matthews
9½" x 11½"   oil   1924

By the mid-twenties, Casson was regularly included on trips with the Group of Seven and in 1926 he was asked to join to replace Frank Johnston. Flattered to be invited, Cass eagerly got up early to light the fire and do the cooking for their weekend excursions (a chore which he continued to assume, according to his artist-friend Clare Bice, who accompanied him for fifteen years on annual outings).

Casson recalled this period of his life in his Convocation Address to the University of Toronto when he was awarded an honourary degree in 1975:

> . . . Jackson, Harris and Carmichael took me along for a two-week sketching trip. This time we camped in a spruce grove on the north shore of Lake Superior to get some protection from the wind. It did not go to zero this time but there was snow every night. Getting up in pitch dark at six in the morning with the tent loaded with snow was a bit of a chore. If we didn't get up at that time we would not be ready to start for the day's work when daylight came. This was only one of such trips and wonderful. I only wish I could take it today.

In the wilderness, the Group took great delight in naming lakes after critics — a beautiful lake for a favourable critic, a smelly, swampy one for a critic whose comments had left a bad odour!

Casson and Carmichael Camp
The McMichael Canadian Collection, Kleinburg, Ontario   8″ x 10¹/₂″   pencil   1928

OLD CHURCH — SWANSEA

In 1917 at the beginning of the Group of Seven fever in Canada, Casson was painting in a traditional manner, realistic landscapes with the paint richly laid on.

Collection of Mr. & Mrs. David Sharpe   9¹/₂″ x 11³/₄″   oil   1920

Cass observed and learned from these artists who had found a new way of looking at the Canadian landscape. Many of his early paintings show how strongly some members of the Group influenced him — Jackson, Carmichael and J. E. H. MacDonald, who, Casson believes, was the most talented member of the Group. It was through association with these men that he was able to develop his own style.

At the end of each day's sketching, they would set out their work around the cabin and praise or comment upon each sketch—but never criticise. It was fertile soil in which to grow.

Because he was so much younger than the members of the original Group, Casson did not have their struggle nor did he suffer the abuse which critics and public heaped on them — but neither did he know their wild elation. The following excerpt from the *Mail and Empire*, dated 8 May, 1926, gives a contemporary viewpoint:

> *The newcomer to the Group of Seven does not experiment with modernism. He is a fine colourist with a feeling for Canadian landscape. To those who know and love the scenery of civilized Ontario, Casson speaks with eloquence. His canvases will form resting places for those who feel nervous irritation when they look upon things they do not understand.*

In 1926 Casson was elected to the Royal Canadian Academy, so that within a matter of months he became a member of the most conservative and the most radical art groups in Canada. He was warned by academicians, "Watch your step, you're keeping bad company."

He managed to keep a foot in both camps, although showing only occasionally with the O.S.A. and the Academy. Mainly he exhibited in the "bad company" of the Group of Seven until its dissolution in 1932.

Meanwhile, A. J. Casson, Frank Carmichael and Fred Brigden founded the Canadian Society of Painters in Water Colour. They wanted to establish this delicate medium as worthy of appreciation for its own sake, not just as a weaker, inferior medium in competition with oils.

The only members of the Group who painted seriously in water colour were Casson, Carmichael and Varley. For Casson, until the 1950s, it comprised three-quarters of his total work. An inexpensive, portable medium, it suited his disciplined, organized way of life. His water colours have a striking clarity and freshness, a greater spontaneity than his large oil canvases — painting for the sheer pleasure of painting, for the sensuous appeal, the almost mystical experience.

Casson thinks this is the advantage of being a "Sunday painter." He painted what he wanted to paint for the joy of it, not because he thought it would sell. But because he was so prolific, the accumulation of his "Sunday paintings" had to be dealt with. Since the opportunities to exhibit were so limited, very few sold.

In the early thirties, Frank and I would get together once a year, we'd weed out our sketches and make a bonfire. There was nothing else to do with them. But you know, I don't think it was such a bad thing. When you painted something you didn't think, "This one will go." You painted because you enjoyed and loved painting.

From the time he moved to Toronto, Casson had been interested in the houses, churches and buildings of the city. One of his early paintings, *Housetops in the Ward* (1924) shows his feeling for the character of structures in their setting. In the thirties, while A. Y. Jackson and Clarence Gagnon were painting the quaint villages of Quebec, he and Carmichael turned to the towns of rural Ontario, where they found inspiration in the picturesque quality of the houses and stores, slumbering in summer heat or in a winter blanket of snow. Casson, especially, had a unique sensitivity to the atmosphere of these small places, where the Depression's impact was less devastating than in the cities. At the same time across the border the American artist Edward Hopper was painting his towns with stark realism. Casson admired his work and into his own scenes has put the same quality of stillness —but it is a peaceful stillness, completely lacking the American's harsh social impact.

In 1932, J. E. H. MacDonald died, Lismer went abroad, Varley moved to Vancouver and the Group of Seven disbanded. It had fulfilled its function by freeing Canadian artists from the limitations and influence of European schools. By that strange fate which in time turns rebels into members of the Establishment, the Group had come to be regarded as the representatives of Canadian art.

A. J. Casson was one of the now-established painters who met with the younger artists to found the Canadian Group of Painters. He was somewhat reluctant, feeling that unless there were a proviso limiting the length of membership to ten years, the new Group would defeat the purpose for which it was formed, which was to help young artists and promote their work. As he feared, the older artists did dominate and so the new Group never did become a spearhead of avant-garde art movements.

NUDE STUDY

In those early years Casson was learning from Harry Britton and Alfred Howell, trying out the palette knife technique of heavy impasto — watching the Group of Seven experiments — and drawing, always drawing. This studio nude exhibits the same swift accuracy which underlies every painting he has done — always first the drawing, because drawing is the grammar of art.

The McMichael Canadian Collection
Kleinburg, Ontario 8½" x 5½" pencil 1917

15

A BREEZY DAY

Around 1900 art nouveau became popular in North America. Its decorative style of sinuous, flat patterns was a reaction to the ugliness of the machine age. In Canada it was quickly adopted by the commercial artists, including most of the future Group of Seven. This is an example of Casson's purely decorative style.

Hart House, University of Toronto   17" x 20"   w.c.   1926

OCTOBER, WHITE RIVER

Telephone poles are the "totems" of northern Ontario, representing the tenuous communication between remote settlements. There is poignancy in this bleak painting of a town already touched by winter, when we consider that in southern Ontario, October is a blaze of autumn foliage and late harvest.

Gift of Mr. & Mrs. J. H. Moore to the Ontario Heritage Foundation   17" x 20"   w.c.   1928

ELORA

While water colour was still his favourite medium, comprising 75 percent of his total output, Casson painted his Elora portfolio, small affectionate "portraits" of an Ontario village, which stand as the pinnacle of his water colour paintings. They show off his skillful draftsmanship, his obsession with fine detail. These sunny water colours contain architectural detail lacking in later work.

Collection of the Artist   17" x 20"   w.c.   1930

BEAVER AND CRANE

Some of the finest commercial art ever produced in Canada came from the hand of A. J. Casson during his forty-three years of work. These are two of a series of animals done for Canada Malting Co. whose president was interested in establishing wild-life preserves across Canada.

Collection of Dr. Steven Demeter   10″ x 8¼″   silk-screen

LAKE KUSHOG Kashagawigamog
Painted the year of his accident, this painting was a break both literally and figuratively from the past. It marked the end of his derivative 19th century technique and the beginning of his own personal 20th century style.

Collection of E. R. Procunier   9³/₈″ x 11¹/₄″   oil   1924

WOODLAND, DEEP BAY, MAGNETAWAN

Here is a spring beechwood with its tracery of light acid-green foliage set against the heavy edging of the trees (undercoat showing through). Casson doesn't like to paint in high summer when heat shimmers the fields and nature is at her most fulsome. More pleasing to him is the haze of autumn or as here, the delicacy of spring.

Collection of E. R. Procunier   9" x 11"   oil   1935

The Fall of France had diminished public enthusiasm for art when A. J. Casson was elected president of the O.S.A. in 1940. To stir up interest, he introduced a special section in the O.S.A. Spring Exhibition — a room devoted to paintings on one subject treated by a number of different artists. The first subject was "war" and Casson arranged for passes to allow the artists into Camp Borden. He himself painted a canvas called *Tanks at Camp Borden*, which was purchased for the archives, and here is his description of his visit to the army camp:

I was never so cold in my life! The temperature was around zero. The C.O. arranged for me to take a ride in a tank and I was stuck up in the turret with the lid open. I couldn't move and just had to stay there getting colder and colder. We were out for four hours and when we got back I headed straight for the canteen. Boy, steaming coffee never tasted so good! But I got the feel of the thing, and an idea of what the boys in the Tank Corps had to put up with.

At Samson-Matthews, Casson was meanwhile proving himself a first-class commercial artist and Charles Matthews, retired president of Samson-Matthews, says of him:

He did a magnificent job. He was one of the top designers. He was a designer more than a painter with us, laying out all kinds of booklets, annual reports, box tops. He did very little in the way of painting — what you'd call landscape painting — for us. But he was one of the finest calligraphers in the country — a most able designer. He didn't do any figure painting — Samson did that, or Sid Hallam ... Frank and Cass were with Samson-Matthews in the heyday of the company. There were Samson, Carmichael, Casson, Gauthier, Shaw, Sid Hallam, Eric Aldwinkle and so many others.

During the early part of the War, artists and art societies were pestered to send exhibitions to officers' messes and armed services stations both in Canada and overseas. This they were loath to do, as the intial experiences proved that the paintings would come back scratched and battered. Then A. Y. Jackson got the idea of having artists donate silk screen designs which could be easily and cheaply printed for distribution to the military bases. He discussed this with Casson who persuaded him to put it into the hands of Samson-Matthews. Charles Matthews and Jackson went to Ottawa and obtained the support of the National Gallery. Matthews next approached business and industry — Canadian Bank of Commerce, Wrigleys, Rowntrees, Canada Packers, Eaton's and others for donations to finance the scheme. The response was splendid and the idea became a reality.

Jackson and Casson arranged for the artists and Casson was responsible for supervising the faithfulness of the reproduction. Artists like Thoreau MacDonald, Charles Comfort, Alan Collier, and Robert Pilot contributed new designs. But later, existing paintings, many by the Group of Seven, were "translated" onto silk screens, one screen for each colour, a complicated process as Casson explains:

You had to get the feel of the painting in a flat colour. A. Y. Jackson, Sid Hallam, Tom McLean and I worked on them. Tom did most of the translations. He was a sidekick of Tom Thomson's in the early days when they were rangers together. But I made the first, the test one, of an old white house in Elora on the main street.

The scheme was a great success. The armed services did not pay anything for the pictures, which were sent express pre-paid because the cost of the reproductions, paid by the sponsors, also included the cost of transportation. Samson-Matthews produced them at cost. There was no profit for anyone. After the armed services' needs were taken care of, the National Gallery produced them for the schools and was thus able to recoup the money it had put into the scheme at the beginning.

Casson was made Vice-president and Art Director of Samson-Matthews in 1946. Although fully occupied with his creative responsibilities, he spent much of his time bringing along the younger artists, as he himself had been encouraged by Ab Robson and Frank Carmichael.

In the mid-forties, there was a radical change in A. J.'s painting style. He was forty-six years old, a restless age, and he was undoubtedly aware of the so-called "quiet revolution" of the Quebec painters like Borduas, Pellan and Riopelle. His landscapes began to take on a strange, nightmarish quality, with elongated forms and stark colours. This led him to experiment in the fifties with planes of light, superimposing images — a double exposure effect — with cool, glacier greens, greys and white. They were very popular:

I did more and went farther and farther with them and suddenly I found they were selling like hotcakes. I felt I had a gimmick and it was working . . . so I just dropped the whole thing.

Drop them he did, and from this experience and his evaluation of it he emerged to greater strength and simplicity—a stripping down of unnecessary detail to clear, basic forms.

23

LUMBERYARD Lake of Two Rivers
This interpretation of clouds is dramatic and three-dimensional, but the artist is beginning to move toward simplified related forms.

Collection of E. R. Procunier   9³/₈″ x 11¹/₄″   oil   1942

FISHERMAN'S POINT

During the war several Canadian artists were asked to make paintings which could be reproduced by the silkscreen method in quantity, to brighten officers' messes at home and overseas. Here we see one which Casson designed, working out his colour areas in careful harmony; white clouds at the top balancing white rock below, flanking the central zigzag area of interlocking shore and water.

The McMichael Canadian Collection, Kleinburg, Ontario   29¹/₄" x 39¹/₄"   tempera on board   1943

CHAIR

For the special section of the O.S.A. show in 1953, eighteen artists were invited to participate in the third event of a series called "The Painter's Art in Laymen's Language." Each artist was asked to interpret the same object, a chair. Casson comments, "It was a Mennonite chair and I was the only one who put it in its proper setting."

Private Collection   20" x 15"   1953

Recognition and honours were beginning to accrue to Casson and in 1948 he was elected president of the Royal Canadian Academy. This same year he was awarded the Province of Ontario Award for *Summer Morning.* Yet he was still painting only in his leisure hours, his working life fully occupied with commercial art.

"All the time Cass was with Samson-Matthews," Charles Matthews recalls, "when he took a holiday he didn't go off somewhere and relax as you or I would. He went painting. This was his idea of a holiday."

Before he retired, Casson never went far afield, except on the occasional assignment. Ontario is his place. He knows and loves the various facets of this province, from its pastoral, rolling countryside where a few houses and stores cluster at a crossroads to form a village, to the craggy heights of lonely lakes where only a loon's cry breaks the stillness. Here he has found all he needs to inspire him, and, like Robert Frost, he sees wonder in the burnished land.

He goes to one place and paints and paints, exploring it thoroughly, coming back time after time to paint it in different seasons, in different weather. Then suddenly he is "painted out." He packs up his paint box and that area is finished as a location for sketching.

"I love travelling, but I can't paint in a strange place. So why run all over?" And yet a series of water colours done when he was in England and Scotland in 1961 are among his finest works. Surprisingly, summer is not his favourite painting season:

> *I like fall and winter. It isn't the colour so much in summer. It's just I've seen so many summer things that are "pretty." There's a sketch I made in England — a water colour — a little place called Weston-on-the-Green, near Woodstock. A village, with thatched cottages. I said to myself, I'm going to paint a thatched cottage that isn't a buckeye. I'm going to try. I worked on that and I got the best sketch I made in England. But you had to leave out the white picket fence and the roses. I killed all that off and I got a good sketch.*

Much fine commercial work came from Casson's fertile brain and skilled hand over the years. He designed two postage stamps, one in 1956 honouring the Pulp and Paper industry and one in 1957 for the Mining industry. He did a series of animal paintings, a set of wild flowers, a series of bird pictures for clients to use as gifts — beautiful pieces of art, flawless in execution and colour. He had the ability, evident even when he was a child, to create within the confines of the assignment, just as the old masters were able to be creative while fulfilling the exacting demands and tastes of their patrons.

In commercial work there are restrictions — a job is given to you. It's a certain size, 8 x 10 maybe. It's a certain subject matter, depending on the product. Then whoever's in charge has figured you can use maybe four colours. Damned good training. It's a discipline. Sid Hallam, the best commercial artist I ever knew, came into my office one day, chewing his pipe. He and I had separate offices. Out in the big room were twelve other artists. Sid said: "I'm sick of listening to those fellows complaining about not having enough colours. Why, you can make a good job in black and white!" You learned to work within limits.

He and Sid kept joint files of magazine clippings:

The polite term was "reference," but we called it "the morgue." I had a cabinet about seven feet high with little trays all the way down full of design and landscapes and all kinds of objects. Sid's was full of figure stuff. We always kept them locked up so other artists wouldn't come in and borrow things and not bring them back. You had to keep things because at three o'clock in the afternoon you might get something to do that needed an invalid in a wheel chair. Well, if you haven't got a reference of a wheel chair, you haven't got time to go hunt one up. We subscribed to dozens of magazines just to tear a few sheets out for our files.

Through the fifties, Casson's paintings were moving towards monumentality, with greater emphasis on pattern. Great rocks looming over his clear lakes were flattened, forming two-dimensional patterns with lowering clouds — simplified, dramatic. His canvases of the La Cloche Mountains are magnificent primeval scenes, with clouds boiling up over tumbled masses of rock.

It was about this time that Casson began to feel that he had exhausted all the angles of commercial art. He was no longer experiencing the same gratification and stimulation from the work.

There was nothing new for me. At a meeting for some new product I knew everything that was going to be said. Commercial art was becoming an assembly line. Back in the forties, Imperial Oil wanted twelve twenty-four-sheet posters for Mobiloil on the theme of animals — elephant for power, etc. — and they handed it to me to do. You made squibs and had them passed. Then one a bit bigger, with more detail. Then the final painting. It was yours, all yours. Now, someone makes up a comprehensive, someone else does this part of the drawing, someone else another part. It's no single person's work.

LUDLOW CASTLE

Casson always insisted he "couldn't paint away from home" (Ontario) but in 1961 when he was sixty-three, he and Margaret went to England and Scotland for the first time. There he found something in the landscape which struck a chord, and the result was a series of beautiful, translucent paintings. He caught the gray mist and the pale sickle greens (so unlike Ontario) and gave these paintings a 19th century character, appropriate to their gentle, ancient settings.

Collection of the Artist   19" x 20"   w.c.   1961

SUNSET, ALGONQUIN PARK

Oxtongue Lake was for years a favourite sketching haunt of A. J. Casson. He said when he was seventy-eight "I could paint Oxtongue today with my eyes closed" but he thinks he may at last have "painted it out." Here is a sunset so spectacular that it is reminiscent of an atomic explosion, a discovery which was still on the scientists' drawing boards in 1942.

Collection of E. R. Procunier   9³/₈" x 11¹/₄"   oil   1942

THUNDERSTORM, WHITNEY

The early 1940s were a time of anguish and of war, and the last of the decade held the uneasiness of postwar reshuffling of people and values. During these years Casson painted a number of dark, brooding scenes in slate tones.

Collection of E. R. Procunier $9^3/_8$" x $11^1/_4$"   oil   1947

SUNLIT ISLE

The first step is the oil sketch done outdoors on the spot. His large paintings usually evolve from sketches he feels need to be worked on. If the sketch is a success, it is likely to remain a small painting, shining with a spontaneity which is sometimes lost in the larger work.

Collection of the Artist
9³/₈" x 11¹/₄"   oil on panel   1975

Back in the studio he makes a scale pencil-drawing of the sketch on paper, the blueprint as it were.

Second stage of 4-stage painting

12" x 15"   pencil

32

Third stage of 4-stage painting

24" x 30"

On the large final canvas he then makes a monochrome underpainting. This is a marvel of delicate understatement in balanced two-dimensional composition containing all the essential forms which will be found in the final painting.

Over the monochrome he lays the final undercoat of either Venetian red or ultra-marine blue, toned up or down with white. It shines around the edges as a luminous foil for his sombre colours and sometimes even through the thin surface paint.

Final stage of 4-stage painting

24" x 30"   oil on canvas

A. J. was also producing in his spare time more paintings than many full-time artists, and the demand for his work was fast increasing. Finally, on New Year's Eve, 1957, he retired from Samson-Matthews after thirty-two years, the last eleven of them as Vice-President and Art Director. He closed his office door for the last time on the last Friday of the year:

On the Monday morning I got up and went up the stairs to my studio and started to paint. People said to me, "You don't have to work like that now." But I had seen too many men right on this street retire and go downhill. I couldn't risk it — and I had an assured thing.

He did indeed. Few Canadians would not be proud to hang a Casson in their homes. Big business has become a patron of the arts and Casson's large canvases decorate the walls of many a boardroom. His earlier works bring unbelievably high prices when they change hands. He just shakes his head: "It's ridiculous!"

The problems many men suffer on retirement have certainly not been Casson's — no moping about the house trying to find little jobs to fill the endless hours. For him, retirement has simply freed him to get on with his real work. He wishes he could have retired ten years earlier.

He still goes off on sketching trips with his wife and comes back with a harvest of sketches which he will sort out in his studio. Some will be developed into large canvases, others, having spontaneously caught the mood of the scene, remain untouched and will be prized by many collectors for their fresh, unstudied beauty.

Much of Casson's time since retirement has been spent in authenticating paintings for individuals, dealers and the police, with whom he has been working to uncover forgeries since 1962. He says there are many good fakes on the market, "I get about one a week to look at. All kinds of stuff is offered at auctions. There's one good rule," he advises. "If the good collectors aren't bidding or the dealers are keeping quiet, keep out of it."

Krieghoff fakes are particularly notorious, and some are so good they can only be detected by tracing their pedigree.

There was a racket some years ago. We could never pin it down. We're pretty sure it was a restorer. You would take on old Krieghoff to him to be restored. He'd say "I'll have to keep it for three or four months, there's so much work to be done." In four months you'd get it back. Looks like a brand new thing! Wonderful job he's done . . . Sure, he'd copied it and kept the original! He disappeared. But any painting with his stamp (showing it had been through his shop) we wouldn't touch with a ten-foot pole.

PICNIC ISLAND
By isolating a single wind-tortured pine tree in Georgian Bay, Casson has symbolized the defiance and endurance of nature in a design of great sweep, excitement and clarity.

Collection of Rosa & Spencer Clark   24" x 30"   oil on panel   1949

There are also some unscrupulous auctioneers. Recently a man called to report his pleasure at having acquired a Casson aquatint, "signed and authenticated." Casson not only informed the man that he had never made an aquatint, but sent the provincial police after the auctioneer. Not long ago, a painting supposedly by Tom Thomson came to him to be checked. The brush strokes were not like Thomson, but any possibility of its authenticity was removed when he looked at the signature. "Thomson" had been spelled with a "p!"

On one occasion, A. J. Casson was himself party to copying the work of another artist. Mr. Spencer Clark of the Guild Inn tells of coming across a large canvas by Lawren Harris. He was most interested in acquiring it, but wanted to be sure it was a genuine Harris. He asked Casson to examine it for him, A. J. assured him it was an original and Clark bought it. For a number of years it hung on the landing of the stairway in the hall of the Guild Inn where it was admired by patrons as they entered the dining room.

Robert McMichael also admired it, and let Mr. Clark know that he thought it should be hanging in the McMichael Canadian Collection.

"But," said Mr. Clark, "it is in a perfect location where it hangs here. My patrons would miss it."

Mr. McMichael was very persistent, however, and finally Mr. Clark decided that if he could get a copy made he would allow the original painting to go to the McMichael Gallery in Kleinburg. He thought immediately of A. J. Casson as the artist to make the copy. Casson agreed to act in an advisory capacity, but suggested Joachim Gauthier do the actual painting. The copy was made a fraction smaller than the original. The circumstances under which it was painted were set down on the back of the canvas and both artists signed it, so that the painting could never be passed off as the original. It is so well executed that, hanging as it does now in the Guild Inn, the keenest viewer could mistake it for Lawren Harris' own work.

Casson's leisure hours are also filled with gardening, with the pleasures of his comfortable home, his devoted family — his daughter, her husband and three grandchildren live close by — and his many friends. He goes down to the Arts & Letters Club for lunch, where he and Charles Matthews are the longest-standing members. He attends openings of exhibitions, is frequently asked to officiate at art functions, adjudicates art shows and is a popular speaker. Recently he was artist-in-residence for a month at a boys' residential school in Quebec.

JOACHIM GAUTHIER'S SKETCH OF A. J. CASSON

When Jo Gauthier completed the sketches of the members for Paul Duval's book, *A Vision of Canada*, he was asked to repaint two of them, the Jackson and Casson. This is the Casson refusé, a sepia drawing here reproduced for the first time.

Collection of E. R. Procunier   16¼" x 13"   pastel & sepia drawing   1965

BON ECHO — Lake Mazinow
This painting, with its thrusting promontory of Bon Echo Rock, is unusually strong for a water colour.

Collection of Rosa and Spencer Clark   11″ x 13″   w.c.   1951

CRESCENDO

The white rocks of the Cloche Hills affected Casson strongly. This painting, so different from his quiet, sunlit villages, supports his contention that he need not go out of his native province to find food for imagination. Colour has been replaced by mood and Wagnerian drama.

Collection of Sarnia Public Library and Art Gallery
Purchased from funds donated by the Industries of Sarnia   30" x 36"   oil on panel   1953

BEECH LEAVES IN WINTER

This small oil, with paint laid on so sketchily that the brush strokes on the prepared board, the pencil sketch and the umber undercoat all show beneath the final painting, is almost a demonstration piece, yet Casson with a few crisp strokes has abstracted the essence of an Ontario beechwood in winter.

Collection of Mrs. James Paterson   12¹/₂″ x 15¹/₂″   oil   undated

40

ROCK STUDY

Casson is able to infuse rocks with as much drama as high mountains. He made several of these pen-and-ink wash drawings and later developed them into dramatic storm paintings, such as *Crescendo* and *Squall on Byng Inlet*.

Gift of Mr. & Mrs. J. H. Moore
to the Ontario Heritage Foundation   11″ x 13¼″   ink drawing   (red & black)   1955

MIST, RAIN AND SUN
Casson's landscapes gradually became more theatrical. His subject matter remained the same but he began to use dramatic spotlighting to isolate a central area. At the same time the clarity of background maintained a two-dimensional effect.

London Public Library and Art Gallery
Gift of Women's Committee   30" x 47¹/₂"   oil   1958

42

The studio where he paints at home is a bright room, built over the garage. It houses an enormous number of paintings in various stages stacked carefully in racks or against the wall on the spotless floor. All the brushes and paints are neatly stored in small drawers beneath his easel. The whole room reflects the orderly character of the man, his disciplined, methodical way of life. One looks in vain for any sign of a passionate splash of paint on floor or wall. It is not his way. Yet the paintings he creates in this room flash with sudden bursts of light, making a magic place, a place without ugliness or torment. And that, in what Toynbee calls our time of troubles, is not to be dismissed lightly.

Awards and honours have been bestowed upon him by art societies, by industry, by his province (a township in the Algoma area has been named after him) by his city. Three universities have conferred honourary degrees. His is a life in which inner fulfillment and public recognition have not compromised his principles nor corrupted his integrity. One can imagine his parents nodding approvingly.

His hundreds of drawings, sketches and paintings, which have recorded the beauty and the character of his land, are a great legacy indeed. But perhaps from a historical point of view A. J. Casson's greatest contribution lies in the present-day link which he provides with that vital period when Canadian art took on its own identity. The Group of Seven laid down the foundations upon which modern art in this country has built, and Casson, although never avant-garde, has made his own unique contribution to the structure. He paints his own vision, unaffected by the tyranny of the new.

VILLAGE AT SUNDOWN

Painting from a sketch of 1920 when the only access to this remote village in Haliburton was by boat, Casson has bathed the scene in a warm autumn haze until it has an ethereal quality, the motionless, timeless beauty of a still-life.

Private Collection   21⅝″ x 25¾″   oil   1960

FARMHOUSE NEAR WIGLE
This painting was in Casson's first one-man show at the Roberts Gallery in Toronto.

Private Collection   24″ x 40″   oil   1960

SILVER MORNING

Note here the latent cubism, the razored tree tops and the white-spined trees.

Collection of Dr. & Mrs. J. G. McMurray   20″ x 24″   oil   1961

LUMBERMAN'S CABIN

"We need the wilderness," Thoreau said, and Casson agrees. Throughout his long painting career he has tramped into the bush to capture on canvas or board the many moods of nature. By a process of reduction he translated what he saw to a simple, individual statement, always beautiful, sometimes dramatic, because that was his vision.

Private Collection   30" x 38"   oil   1971

COUNTRY STORE
In this late work Casson has painted a familiar village scene with its single figure. But volumes have become flat planes, with coloured shapes on cutout houses. There is no longer dramatic high-lighting.

Collection of the Artist   20″ x 24″   oil on panel   1972

Methods and Effects

When A. J. Casson began to paint in oils, he was already under the influence of the Group of Seven, most of whom had studied in Europe. They were affected in style by the Impressionists and the Post-Impressionists, and in style and content by the Scandinavians who held an exhibition in Buffalo in 1913. They digested these influences and developed their own dynamic style in their search for a truly Canadian art. The effects of the European schools had already been filtered through the strong personalities of the Group before they reached Casson. It is impossible, therefore, to trace a Van Gogh effect or a Fauves technique in his work. But it is easy to see that Jackson, MacDonald, Carmichael were his teachers and his constant companions in his formative years.

For a short time, in his desire to imitate them, he laid on his paint very thickly, with short strokes of the brush. But, he admits:

I can't build paint up. I've never consciously drifted away from it. I use solid paint but I lay it on smoothly. The heavy build-up was for textural effects in the old days.

But he never achieved the wild colour or the joyous abandon of a Tom Thomson or an A. Y. Jackson, nor was he impelled by their fierce patriotism.

Today he uses oils almost like water colours, very thinly. Far from wanting texture now, his flattened planes and two-dimensional effects are achieved with thin applications of pure colour. He just roughs in the basic composition and then begins to sketch, on the spot, in oil or water colour. The sketches he selects to finish into large canvases are usually ones he was not too happy about: "Usually a bad sketch with a good idea. One you can get your imagination working on." Generally the painting develops successfully, but occasionally:

There was one called First Snow — the leaves in full colour in autumn and then a fall of wet snow on them. The next day it was gray. I did my sketch and then came right home and painted. It was awful! I just turned it to the wall. Six months went by and then one day I was looking for something and I accidentally turned it around. I could see what was wrong. I painted the whole thing over with a palette knife and it came off. I don't like an oil that goes wrong and you have to flounder with it. Don't muck around with it. Get a new panel or scrape it off and start over. If you overwork a thing, you lose something. If I find I'm having trouble I just take a month off and work in the garden and I come back refreshed.

Casson never uses photographs for his paintings. He might occasionally take one of a house to record some detail of a window or decorative gable, but never of landscape. He does not need them. His mind is so trained that he has almost total recall.

"If you asked me to paint a picture of Oxtongue Lake with one of the islands, I could sit down and do it right now."

He believes he can tell when an artist has worked from a photograph: "There's one well-known painter, now dead. You look at his later canvases and you can see photograph written all over them. He was too good an artist to do the things he did if he wasn't slavishly following a photograph."

Even for a vision as ephemeral as a cloud bank, he will not resort to photography. He "works like mad" to try to capture the effect on the spot and usually he succeeds.

It is in his colour sense that Casson's greatest strength lies. His colours induce the magic in his paintings. He uses a simple scheme, a restricted palette.

I've never liked using every colour of the rainbow. Before I start a canvas I have a definite colour scheme in mind. In Old Mill at Cheltenham I used only gray, white, green and pink as the basic scheme, with a few specks of others for accent. One day I saw the Velasquez painting of Phillip IV of Spain. The only discernible colours were black, brown, silver and rose. That started me on simple, restricted colour schemes . . . Lawren Harris and Carmichael always worked to a scheme too. In 1917 I took lessons from Harry

Britton and he taught me that if you go out up north on a gray day you don't load up your palette with cadmium orange, brilliant yellows and that sort of thing. If you do, you're going to waste so much time dirtying them. You use yellow ochre. The only thing is, if you have a good thing working, you have to be careful not to overdo it.

But whether in the brilliant tones of Credit Forks 1930 or the cool marine greens and pale golds of his abstracts of the fifties, his understanding and use of colour is unerring — clean and clear, the tonal values perfectly balanced.

Casson's water colours are considered by some his finest works. They are crisp and defined. They have the clarity of a spring morning. His colours are never harsh or raw, never muddied. And these paintings have a spontaneity and a sparkle which is lacking in most of his large oil canvases. Unlike many water colourists, David Milne for example, he does not often use the white paper as part of the painting. He covers the surface sometimes almost indiscernibly, giving the white a faint cast of yellow, or grey, which can only be seen on very close inspection. There is a holiday feeling about the water colours he painted in England and Scotland — a free joyousness seldom found in his other works.

One could trace the development of A. J. Casson's art by examining his paintings of houses and stores. In *Old House Haliburton* he has

FIRST SNOW

Searching for a new style, Casson for a while painted distorted romantic visions of dream worlds. Of this work he says "I came right home and painted it. It was just awful! So I turned it to the wall. I guess six months went by. One Sunday I turned it round. I could see what was wrong and I painted the whole thing with a palette knife in one day over top of it. I don't like overworking a thing — you lose something."

Art Gallery of Hamilton, Gift of Mrs. H. H. Leather   30" x 36"   oil on masonite   1962

CREDIT FORKS

This is one of the artist's finest water colours in a period of prolific production. He has succeeded, with his strange "cloud-sitter" perspective, in drawing the viewer down into the Credit Valley, by placing the horizon at the top of the picture.

Art Gallery of Ontario
Gift from Friends of Canadian Art Fund, 1930   16$^7/_8$" x 20$^3/_{16}$"   w.c.   1930

OLD HOUSE, HALIBURTON

This painting, exhibited at the Canadian National Exhibition in 1930, is strong and monumental for a water colour. One of the early "portrait" paintings, it does not have the usual clouds and the artist's two-dimensional treatment creates the effect of flat, even lighting of studio photography.

Private Collection   17″ x 20″   w.c.   1927

SUMMER SUN

Casson was expanding his ideas in the late thirties, zeroing in on southern Ontario with the obvious exhilaration of discovery. He would soon move on into a geometric phase. But here he is still involved with architectural detail, with people and animals and human activity. His houses had vines and his windows were to see through. This is as close to narrative painting as he ever allowed himself. It was his Diploma piece for membership in the Royal Canadian Academy.

The National Gallery of Canada, Ottawa   30" x 36"   oil on canvas   1939

54

ANTIQUE STORE

What Casson *saw* was an unremarkable building of artificially weathered pine, with clutter overflowing the verandah onto the trampled yard. What he *recorded* was quite a different matter. His trained eye enabled him to "skim off all the junk" as he said, leaving bare, two-dimensional design, a symbolic stage.

Collection of the Artist   30" x 36"   oil   1974

carefully painted the portrait of a house, realistic but picturesque against a rural background of lake and hill. In the thirties, in his Elora series, he painted colourful vignettes of village life — the four corners, a drowsy street, an isolated store — using the buildings to give character to the scene. This narrative phase reached its climax in his diploma piece for the Royal Canadian Academy in 1940, *Summer Sun*. In this genre painting the houses are occupied — we can see several of the villagers sweeping, lounging, walking, while the chickens peck about in the yard. Then in the mid-forties he began his experiments in abstract surrealism. His houses became wooden blocks with exaggerated elongated shapes with patches of colour to suggest windows, as in *First Snow*, 1952. Great planes of light and dark were used to heighten the sinister stillness. He dropped this style when he felt it was becoming "gimmicky" and turned again toward realism, now idealizing the typical frame farmhouses of Ontario with their neo-Gothic painted dormers and decorated barge boards. Mainly white clapboard, they stand clean, full-faced in the middle ground of the canvas, almost like a frieze painting but without the depth of relief. As in *Farmhouse near Wigle*, they are flat, dead-centered, with the timeless quality of monuments. In the *Antique Store*, 1974 the building fills the whole canvas. There is no attempt to put it in a village, nor to people it. It has been stripped of all unessential details. On the porch are placed one or two antiques selected from the clutter of the actual store. The effect is flat, two-dimensional, simplified, dramatic — like a stage setting. It is a masterpiece of design.

Casson's innate sense of design, combined with his commercial training, are evident in the harmony of his composition. One can cover half of almost every painting and find that the other half will stand alone. This balance and control are his strength and perhaps his limitation. But through them he has been able to create that sense of stillness so characteristic of all his work, that sense of a moment crystalized, time arrested. Of this stillness, Casson says: "It's like when you're out and it's been snowing. It's quieter than quiet."

There is an appeal in Casson's work because of its detachment from the strife and ugliness of life. He preaches no sermon, makes no social comment. He does not probe our guilty motives nor make us feel ashamed. He simply distills for us a scene of primordial beauty or monumental calm and offers it to us as a purely aesthetic experience.

Malraux has said, "Art has nothing to serve and nothing to prove but the transcending existence of beauty . . . It finds its end when it tears men away from the human condition and gives them access to the sacred condition . . . This is why at all times, when art reached its highest levels, it has had a static character, a god-like immobility."

Chronology

Alfred Joseph Casson, Born 17 May, 1898, in Toronto.

1907 – Moved to Guelph with family.
1912 – Moved to Hamilton with family.
1913 – Employed at Laidlaw Lithographing Co. (first job)
1916 – Moved to Toronto with family.
1917 – First painting exhibited, C.N.E.
1919 – Employed by Rous and Mann.
1921 – Exhibited with O.S.A.
1923 – Member of O.S.A., exhibited at National Gallery.
1924 – Married Margaret Purdy.
1925 – Founding member of Canadian Society of Painters in Water Colour; member of Group of Seven.
1926 – Member of R.C.A.; joined Samson Matthews.
1932 – Group of Seven disbanded.
1933 – Founding member of Canadian Group of Painters.
1940 – President, O.S.A; bronze medal, International Business Machines Ltd.

1941 – Victory Loan award.
1946 – Vice-President and Art Director of Samson Matthews.
1948 – Province of Ontario award.
1955 – Vice-President Art Gallery of Toronto (later Art Gallery of Ontario).
1956 – Designed stamp honouring Pulp & Paper Industry.
1957 – Designed stamp honouring Mining Industry; gold medal, University of Alberta; retired from Samson Matthews.
1960 – Chairman of Art Committee of O'Keefe Centre.
1962 – Consultant to Ontario Provincial Police on fraudulent art.
1967 – Silver Centennial Medal.
1970 – R.C.A. Medal; honourary degree, University of Western Ontario.
1971 – Honourary Degree, University of Saskatchewan.
1973 – Fellow, Ontario College of Art.
1975 – Honourary Degree, University of Toronto.

Selected Bibliography

Buchanan, Donald W., *The Growth of Canadian Painting*, London: Collins, 1950.

Canadian Painters, Donald W. Buchanan ed., Phaidon Press, 1945, p. 18.

Colgate, William, *Canadian Art, Its Origin and Development*, Toronto: Ryerson Press, 1943, p. 104.

Duval, Paul, *A. J. Casson*, Toronto: privately printed 1975.

Duval, Paul, *Alfred Joseph Casson*, Toronto: Ryerson Press, 1951.

Duval, Paul, *Canadian Water Colour Painting*, Toronto: Burns & MacEachern, 1954.

Duval, Paul, *Group of Seven Drawings*, Toronto: Burns & MacEachern, 1965, Plates 62, 63.

Harper, J. Russell, *Painting in Canada*, Toronto: University of Toronto Press, 1966.

Housser, Frederick, *Amateur Movement in Canadian Painting*, Yearbook of the Arts in Canada, Toronto: Macmillan & Co., 1929.

MacDonald, Colin A., *A Dictionary of Canadian Artists*, Ottawa, Vol. 1, 1967.

Reid, Dennis, *A Concise History of Canadian Painting*, Toronto, Oxford University Press, 1973. Also, exhibition catalogues and newspaper articles since 1921.

58

Printed and Bound in Hong Kong